TAEKWONDO
in a week

David Mitchell

Headway · Hodder & Stoughton

ACKNOWLEDGEMENTS

The author and publisher gratefully acknowledge the contribution made by members of the British JidoKwan under the technical supervision of their principal, Ian Morrison, to the production of this book. The British JidoKwan headquarters is at 38 Bracewell Road, London W10 6AF.

British Library Cataloguing in Publication Data
Mitchell, David
    Taekwondo in a week.
    I. Title
    796.8

ISBN 0 340 56421 0

First published 1992

© 1992 David Mitchell

Typeset by Rowland Phototypesetting Ltd, Bury St Edmunds, Suffolk. Printed in Hong Kong for the educational publishing division of Hodder and Stoughton Ltd, Mill Road, Dunton Green, Sevenoaks, Kent by Colorcraft Ltd.

CONTENTS

INTRODUCTION

Taekwondo is a Korean word made from **tae** meaning 'foot', **kwon** meaning 'fist' and **do** meaning 'path' or 'way that you should follow'. So taekwondo means 'way of the foot and fist'.

Taekwondo uses the hands and feet to deliver high energy impact techniques.

We know from ancient records that the first systematised development of Eastern martial art began in China. From there it spread to Korea, Okinawa and Japan through the activities of Chinese military attachés and Buddhist monks.

We also know that Buddhist monks travelled a great deal and some of them may have come from the famous monastery at Shaolin, where martial art practice was studied and refined.

Korean martial artists seemed to prefer kicks above hand techniques. Perhaps they had learned a Northern Chinese system in which leg techniques were stressed. But even if they did, their own development far surpasses that of the founders and taekwondo kicks are now widely recognised as the most sophisticated to be found in any martial art anywhere in the world.

Another characteristic of Korean martial art practice is its insistence on testing the power of techniques against wood, bricks and tile.

So whatever its origins, taekwondo is now a uniquely Korean martial art.

Taekwondo is the national sport of Korea and it is taught both in schools and in the armed services. The latter connection allows us to legitimately call taekwondo 'a martial art' – something we cannot do with many other Far Eastern systems.

The different types of taekwondo

Taekwondo is actually an umbrella term for a number of different Korean fighting systems which united together around 1955. At first, each system remained distinct but all have since merged into a single common practice. As you might imagine, unification was not achieved without alienating some instructors and consequently, there are at least two international governing bodies.

By far the larger and more prominent is the World Taekwondo Federation (WTF), based in Seoul. WTF has been recognised by the International Olympic Committee but at the time of writing, taekwondo has not yet been accepted into the actual Games. The International Taekwondo Federation (ITF) is the only rival organisation of note. However this group is far smaller and is unlikely ever to achieve any comparable level of recognition.

INTRODUCTION

WTF Taekwondo has therefore been given pride of place in this book, though the techniques described are common to both. The major difference between the two lies in the form of competition practised. WTF Taekwondo contestants wear padded jackets and headguards because they use full power kicks and punches to the head and body.

Additionally, WTF competition is held over a number of rounds, so contestants must be capable of maintaining a constant and effective barrage of technique throughout. This makes severe demands on physical fitness and is the reason why this book contains an appropriate training programme.

ITF Taekwondo is the longer established of the two and it does not use padded jackets or headguards in its competitions. Instead, contestants wear padded boots and gloves, restricting the level of impact to what we might call 'semi contact'.

How taekwondo is practised

Both forms of taekwondo are practised according to a rigid syllabus which begins with the core techniques of the system. These punches, strikes and kicks are the alphabet of taekwondo from which 'words' are made up. The words are what we call 'combination techniques' and, continuing the analogy further, words are assembled into sentences through the practice of what are called 'patterns'. These link whole series of techniques into a coherent whole.

It is not enough to develop a single deadly blow – what happens if it misses? You must learn how to strike many times, to different targets and from different positions. This is the key to effective taekwondo.

This book will try to cover most aspects of taekwondo training, first teaching basic techniques and then going on to combinations. Unfortunately the very nature of patterns makes them difficult to include within this type of book.

We next look at pre-arranged sparring as a safe way of testing techniques in a realistic situation, and then go on to complete the week with competition.

A typical WTF grading system

Your training will be marked at regular intervals by grading examinations. Think of these as rungs in a ladder of progression up which you climb on your way to the coveted black belt.

Each grade is identified by a coloured belt, and consists of a quota of techniques which you must learn to perform to an acceptable skill standard. Assuming that you train twice a week, then grading examinations will crop up every three to four months.

INTRODUCTION

The following belt colours are typical of the British WTF grading system:

1 White belt
3 Yellow belt
5 Green belt
7 Blue belt
9 Red belt
11 Black belt first dan

2 White belt with yellow tab
4 Yellow with green tab
6 Green with blue tab
8 Blue with red tab
10 Red with black tab

Grading intervals between the black belt dan grades are measured in years, rather than months and the highest grade that can be awarded is 9th dan.

How to find a good taekwondo club

Many people think that if someone is wearing a black belt, then they must be both technically expert and socially responsible. This, unfortunately, is not the case! It is possible for a student of taekwondo to leave after reaching only a low level of skill, to buy a black belt and then to open a club teaching beginners such as YOU. Imposing looking certificates need only mean that the person has access to a good printer!

It is therefore essential that anyone thinking of taking up taekwondo checks out prospective clubs before they join.

Naturally no-one would expect a novice to be able to tell good taekwondo from bad – and that is why responsible coaches have banded together to form a governing body which is in membership of the Martial Arts Commission (MAC).

If your local club is listed on the MAC's register of approved clubs, then its technical standards are above a minimum level. Moreover, its coaches will have had to pass a stringent MAC Coaching Assessment to ensure that they are able to teach efficiently and safely.

By joining a MAC recognised club, you will have access to an individual insurance policy which provides both personal accident coverage and a third party indemnity. Furthermore, the grading awards which you receive will be recognised throughout Britain, meaning that you can transfer freely between clubs without loss of technical recognition.

So find out whether your local club is recognised by writing to the Martial Arts Commission, 15–16 Deptford Broadway, London SE8 4PE and be sure to enclose a self addressed return envelope. Alternatively, telephone the Commission during office hours on 081 691 3433. If you live outside Britain, then contact your national sports agency for the address of your taekwondo governing body.

INTRODUCTION

Costs of participation in taekwondo

The first cost any new student has to face is paying for membership to the selected club. Usually one composite annual fee is charged and this includes affiliation to the governing body and the Martial Arts Commission. Expect to pay between £7–£25 for annual membership and registration.

You will also have to pay a nightly training fee to cover the coach's cost in renting premises. This can be as little as 50 pence or as much as £3. Finally, grading examinations may be free, or they may cost up to £10 for coloured belt grades. So check all these costs out before you join.

The taekwondo training tunic consists of a white polycotton jacket and trousers secured by a coloured belt. Few general sports shops can supply proper tunics and while you can make do with a more readily available karate suit, you should try to get the right equipment. This will either be available through the club itself, or the coach will give you the address of a specialist supplier.

Expect to pay between £15–£60 for a uniform, depending upon its quality. Novices should always opt for the cheaper tunic since this will more than last them through their first year of training. Select one size larger than you need because they shrink steadily with the regular weekly washing needed to preserve hygiene.

If you join a WTF club, you may also be expected to buy the padded jackets and headguard. These are expensive! However, most good clubs keep spare equipment which you can use and in any case, you won't be doing any free sparring for a while!

You might also care to invest in special lightweight trainers which protect the feet from injury. You can't use normal trainers because their method of fastening might cause injury to your partner and anyway, they are too stiff to allow you to form the various foot weapons needed.

ITF clubs will expect you to buy your own fist and feet protectors but again, you won't need these for some time after joining.

Buy a large sweatshirt that you can slip over the top of your tunic. This is useful during warming-up before the lesson proper starts, and for any lulls in training.

INTRODUCTION

Getting ready to train

Taekwondo makes demands upon the body in terms of physical fitness. Prepare to meet these demands by means of a 10–20 minute warm-up. Warming-up consists of moving the body and limbs through their full range of movement by means of a series of exercises. These start off slowly but become more vigorous as you work up a sweat.

Choose activities such as running or jumping on the spot, followed by arm-circling and trunk twisting. Avoid unduly stretching your joints until later in the evening, when your muscles are warm and relaxed.

Warm-down at the end of the training session, gradually slowing the pace of your exercises until you are ready to get changed. A good warm-down allows a continuing blood flow to clear away all the fatigue-producing by-products of muscle activity. This in turn means less stiffness in the days following.

Etiquette

Taekwondo practice begins and ends with courtesy. This is as well because the techniques taught are extremely forceful and might prove dangerous if the student has no self discipline. It is essential that all students of taekwondo take this point seriously. Show respect for your teacher, from whom your better understanding of taekwondo will come. Show respect also to your classmates and treat them in the way you yourself would want to be treated.

Express this respect by means of a standing bow to the coach when entering or leaving the training hall. Pause on entering and face the coach. Draw your heels together and allow your arms to hang naturally at your sides. Close your hands into fists. This is 'attention stance'. Make a standing bow by inclining your head and upper body forward, pause briefly at the lowest point and then straighten up again.

If you arrive late, then wait to be invited to train by the coach or senior student – don't just barge in. Whenever the coach speaks, stop what you are doing and pay close attention. Do not leave the training hall without the coach's permission and do not smoke or lark about. Practise only the techniques you are shown and do not be tempted to experiment.

You are now ready to begin the week's training!

BASIC TECHNIQUES

Making a fist

The first thing to learn is how to make an effective fist. Begin by opening your hand out fully. Then:

- curl the fingers down so they touch the pad of flesh running along the top of the palm;

- fold the fingers forward from the knuckles;

- lock the fist closed by folding your thumb across the index and middle fingers (Figure 1).

Do not enclose your thumb within your fist because if you do, a hard impact may well dislocate it!

Strike the target with the index and middle finger knuckles only, holding the fist in such a way that the wrist doesn't flex painfully on impact.

Figure 1   Roll your fingers into the palm of your hand and lock the fist closed with your thumb.

9

MONDAY

Learn how to use your fist by asking your partner to put on a padded sparring jacket. Then punch lightly against it. If you are doing it correctly, then your two large knucles will become red. Try punching a little harder as you become more confident, to see whether your wrist joint is properly set up.

Trouble Shooting

Problems
The middle joints of your fingers make first contact.

Resolutions
Keep striking a target and your fist profile will improve. Alternatively you can do press-ups on your knuckles.

The thumb is hurt by the impact.

Did your thumb point forward, or did you enclose it in the fist? Close it tightly over the fingers.

Your wrist bends painfully on impact.

You haven't lined up your wrist joint correctly.

Punching techniques

Once you can make a good fist, the next stage is to learn how to throw it.

Lunge punch

Lunge punch is a very basic way of practising the mechanism of punching. Begin by taking up attention stance, then step out to the side with your left and right legs until their outer edges are about a shoulder-width apart. Your feet are parallel to each other in what is known as 'ready stance'. Then:

- step forward a good pace-and-a-half with your left leg;

- your left foot points directly ahead, the rear foot is as close to pointing straight ahead as you can get it without bending the knee;

- straighten your right knee fully;

- bend your left knee so it overlies your instep;

- twist your hips forward, so they both face the front;

- extend your left arm forward and straighten the elbow, turning your fist palm-downwards;

- bend your right elbow and hold your fist palm-upwards just above your belt (Figure 2).

MONDAY

Figure 2   Turn your hips forward, straighten your back leg, extend your left arm and pull the right back to your side.

Figure 3   Don't move your arms as you step forward.

This posture is known as 'forward stance'. Then:

- step forward with your right foot;
- don't move your arms as the right foot takes up position (Figure 3);
- pull back your left fist and punch with the right;
- rotate both fists, so the right turns palm-downwards and the left palm-upwards;
- spasm-close both fists on impact.

Lunge punch develops power through the long stepping movement but in order to harness this, you must punch at exactly the right time. Punch too early and you will throw yourself forward and off balance. Punch too late and you will lose the energy of body movement.

Trouble Shooting

Problems
Your punch is not powerful.

Resolutions
Did you pull back the other fist strongly enough? Was your body weight moving forward as the punch connected?

Your punch lacks penetration.

Check whether your leading knee is well bent.

You bob up and down as you step.

Keep your knees bent as you move between stances.

Reverse punch

Reverse punch is similar to lunge punch except that if the left foot leads, then the punch is made with the right fist – and vice versa. Begin from left foot forward stance and extend your left fist. Then, without stepping forward, punch with your right and pull your left fist back quite strongly.

Once you are in this position, you can perform successive reverse punches each time you step forwards.

Re-read the section on lunge punch/trouble shooting and in addition:

Trouble Shooting

Problems	Resolutions
Your shoulder leads and your stance is unstable.	You have overtwisted your hips. They must face square-on to the front.
Your punch lacks impact.	Check that your weight moved forward and that your front knee overlies the instep.

The jab

The jab is a short, jolting punch delivered with the lead hand.

Begin from ready stance by stepping forward a pace with your left foot and:

- point your leading foot forward and turn the trailing foot 45 degrees outwards;

- retain the original width of ready stance;

- raise your left arm and bend the elbow 90 degrees, so the fist is about shoulder height and the elbow is close to the ribs. This is your forward guard hand;

- raise your right arm and bring the fist close to your chest. This is your trailing guard hand;

You have now taken up 'walking stance' (Figure 4). This is a general purpose stance from which fast moves can be made in any direction.

The jab will be made with the leading left fist, so:

- slide your left foot forward a half pace, so the stance lengthens slightly;

- bend both knees slightly and lower your centre of gravity;

- move your right fist forward by a few centimetres;

MONDAY

Figure 4   In walking stance, one foot leads the other and the fists are held in a guard position.

Figure 5   Draw back your right fist and simultaneously snap punch with the left.

- then pull your right fist back hard to your chest and use this action to help thrust out a sharp punch with your left fist (Figure 5);
- tighten your fist as impact is about to be made, and rotate your forearm so the palm faces downwards;
- allow natural joint elasticity to snap the spent punch back into forward guard position.

Trouble Shooting

Problems	**Resolutions**
The punch was weak.	Did you co-ordinate the slide forward with the jab? Did you pull back your lead guard hand and spasm-close your fist on impact? Did you move your shoulder behind the action?
The spent punch came back slowly.	Retrieve the jab quickly, using natural muscular elasticity.

You can extend the range of your jab by leaning forward slightly, but avoid leading with your chin.

Practical reverse punch

Practical reverse punch is similar to the jab except that it always uses the trailing guard hand. Begin from left walking stance and:

- slide forward a half pace;
- move your bodyweight over the front foot;
- draw back your left fist;
- twist your right hip forwards and thrust out your right fist;
- twist your right forearm palm-downwards and spasm-close the fist on impact (Figure 6).
- draw back the spent punch and reinstate the forward guard hand.

Reverse punch is more powerful than snap punch because of the greater hip involvement, stronger shoulder movement and longer punching action. Bodyweight travels forward behind the punch to the extent that the rear foot may lift from the mat.

14

Figure 6   Power reverse punch with a combination of hip twist and pull-back of the non-punching fist.

MONDAY

Trouble Shooting	
Problems	**Resolutions**
The punch is weak.	Most common cause is a failure to combine powerful hip twist with strong pull back of the leading guard hand. Another cause is failure to move bodyweight forward behind the punch.
Pull back of the spent fist is slow.	Speed things up by thrusting your guard hand forwards.

There is no need to slide forward in order to perform either snap or reverse punch. It's just that the slide forward closes range and adds more power to the punching action.

Snap punch/reverse punch combination

Now you know how to throw practical punches, practise with your partner, taking it in turns to pummel the padded jackets with jabs and reverse punches. When you feel comfortable with these two techniques, try doing one and then the other immediately after, in a sort of 'one-two' action.

Slide forward from left walking stance and:

- jab his jacket hard with your leading left fist;
- pull the spent fist back quickly and use this action to help thrust out a powerful reverse punch;
- pull the spent punch back quickly and move to a different position. Then repeat the sequence.

Aim to hit the jacket with two resounding impacts in quick succession. Change the starting stance so you snap punch with the right fist and reverse punch with the left. And when you get really confident, have your partner move around slowly, to get you used to ranging on a moving target.

MONDAY

Basic blocking techniques

Blocking techniques interrupt an incoming fist or foot and stop them from hitting their intended target. Blocks form part of the basic syllabus of taekwondo.

Head block

Head block uses a rising and rotating forearm to deflect the opponent's punch upwards and away from your face. Begin from ready stance, then step forwards into left forward stance. Lift your left arm and bend the elbow, so the forearm protects your forehead. Then rotate your forearm so the little finger part of the fist faces upwards. Carry your right fist palm-upwards on the hip (Figure 7). Practise further head blocks by:

- stepping into right forward stance;
- dropping your left forearm down;
- bringing your right forearm up the outside of the left (Figure 8);
- pulling the left fist back to the hip and thrusting up with the right fist into a new head block.

Head block is made more powerful by the pulling back of the previous block, so synchronise this with the forward movement of your body.

Figure 7   Head block presents an angled forearm so as to deflect the incoming attack.

Figure 8   Your forearms momentarily cross in front of your upper body.

Figure 9   The opponent's face punch is deflected upwards.

Test the effectiveness of your head block by facing your partner in ready stance. Your partner steps into right forward stance and you step back with your left foot into the same. Then your partner steps forward and attempts to lunge punch you in the face. Match his movement exactly, stepping back smoothly and head blocking with your left arm (Figure 9).

Trouble Shooting

Problems
The opponent's punch hits you before you have chance to block.

Resolutions
You blocked too slowly. Begin the block even as he begins his step forwards.

The opponent's punch hits you in the forehead.

Use the block to lift the punch clear of your forehead.

MONDAY

Figure 10 Look over your shoulder, lift your right heel and slide your foot across the floor.

It goes without saying that both students must co-operate. The attacker must only move as fast as the defender can cope with, and the punch must be controlled to avoid risk of injury. Later, when skill levels have improved, it will be possible to punch and block quite quickly, several times in succession.

This is a useful training drill because it teaches you the concepts of timing and distance. Move too slowly and the opponent will overtake you. Take too great a step back and there will be no need to block the opponent's punch.

Also practise head block in conjunction with a turn. Begin from, say, left forward stance with the left arm extended in lunge punch. Then:

- raise your heel and slide the right foot across (Figure 10);

- swivel your hips strongly and about face;

- perform head block with your right forearm.

The trick is to block as you are turning, not afterwards.

Trouble Shooting

Problems	Resolutions
Your new stance is too narrow.	You didn't step far enough across.
Your new stance is too wide.	You stepped too far across.
Your new stance is too high.	You drew your rear leg up as you stepped across.
You bobbed up as you turned.	You straightened your knees as you turned.

MONDAY

Only experience will tell you how far to step across with your trailing foot.

Remember to slide your trailing foot over the floor – don't lift it!

Low block

This technique also uses the forearm, but this time in a downswinging arc that knocks an attacking front kick to the side. Begin from left forward stance and extend your left arm downwards until it is just above and to the side of the left knee. Then:

- step forward into right forward stance;

- as you step, extend your left arm downwards and fold the right across your chest, so the little finger edge of the fist is just above your left shoulder (Figure 11);

- then strongly draw back your left fist to the hip and block downwards with your right arm.

This block is also powered by the pulling back of the non-blocking arm.

Figure 11   Bring your right arm to the top of your left shoulder whilst extending the left forwards and down.

Trouble Shooting

Problems
The block finishes to the inside of your leading knee.

Resolutions
Continue the block so it completes slightly to the outside of your leading knee.

The blocking fist is well above the leading knee.

The blocking fist should only be slightly above the leading knee.

Practise low block in conjunction with a turn by treating the slide across of the trailing foot as though it was a step forward.

Kicking techniques

Front kick

Front kick generally uses the ball of the foot to strike the opponent but before you can use it, you need to practise pulling the toes back. A correct foot shape has the instep in line with the shin (Figure 12). Most novices either fail to pull their toes back, or they drop their heels too low, so impact force is wasted when the ankle flexes.

Practise getting the correct foot shape by kicking against a padded target.

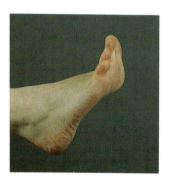

Figure 12   Fully extend your instep and pull back the toes.

Trouble Shooting

Problems	Resolutions
You hurt your toes on impact.	Pull your toes back.
You hit the target with the sole of your foot.	Bring your instep into line with the shin.

When you can form the correct foot shape, take up left walking stance and then slide your foot forward slightly whilst bending your knees. Maintain the same guard. You are now in fighting stance.

Fighting stance is especially useful for performing kicks because the bent knees allow you to explode into action without any telltale shifting of weight. Perform front kick by:

- turning your left leg slightly outwards;

- changing your guarding hands, so the right now leads;

- bringing your right foot forward and up, so it passes close by the left knee;

MONDAY

- lifting your right knee higher than the target (Figure 13);

- then dropping your knee as you thrust out the lower leg (Figure 14);

- retrieve the spent kick and set it down carefully in right fighting stance.

Lean back slightly as you kick, so as to counterbalance the weight of the extending leg.

Trouble Shooting

Problems

You moved your body forward as you lifted your kicking knee.

You opened your groin as you lifted your kicking knee.

You bobbed up and down as you kicked.

Your foot skated up the front of the target pad.

Resolutions

Take up a shorter, higher opening stance.

Take your kicking foot close by the knee of your supporting leg.

Keep your supporting knee bent throughout.

You didn't raise your knee and then drop it, so as to thrust the foot out.

Repeat the kick on alternate legs, then practise against your partner, kicking his padded jacket with a succession of front kicks.

Figure 13   Raise your kicking knee higher than the target . . .

Figure 14   . . . and drop it as you thrust the foot out.

Figure 15   Thrust kick high into the opponent's padded jacket, where it is more difficult to apply a block.

Thrusting front kick

Thrusting front kick uses the sole of the foot to drive the opponent back, or to prevent him from rushing in. Begin from fighting stance and:

- bring your right foot forward as before;
- raise the kicking knee high and bring it close to your chest;
- then arch your back and thrust out your foot, striking the opponent solidly in the centre of his padded jacket with the sole of your foot (Figure 15).

Recoil from this technique can be quite substantial, so move your body behind the kicking action.

Roundhouse kick

Roundhouse kick also uses the ball of the foot, though it is possible to strike with the instep. Begin from left fighting stance and:

- twist your supporting foot outwards slightly;
- change your guarding hands;
- pick up your right foot and bring it around and forwards;
- swivel on your supporting foot and take your right knee across the front of your body (Figure 16);
- thrust your kicking foot out and strike the side of the target (Figure 17);
- withdraw the spent kick and set it down carefully.

For best effect, the kicking foot should rise above the target and then drop down onto it.

Figure 16   Swivel on the supporting foot and bring your kicking knee across the front of your body.

Figure 17   Thrust your instep hard into the side of the opponent's head.

MONDAY

Trouble Shooting

Problems	Resolutions
You kicked diagonally upwards.	You failed to turn your hips fully into the kick.
The kick was low.	Lift your kicking knee until it points at the target.

Roundhouse kick uses a great deal of hip twist and your supporting foot may turn a complete 180 degrees during its execution.

An aerobic training programme

Now we have experience of some basic techniques, it becomes possible to design a suitable aerobic training programme. Such a programme will provide a basic fitness platform on which we can build our specific requirements.

Remember, improvement in taekwondo comes about through increase in skill, and increase in skill only comes about through countless repetitions. Since you need to be fit to repeat techniques many times over, then it follows that you must have a certain level of fitness in order to improve.

The aerobic training programme will take up about 12–20 minutes of your day and on training nights you can use it as a warm-up.

Begin by shadow punching against a mirror or a light suspended bag. Snap and reverse punch in rapid succession, combining these with quick foot movements, so you weave and bob as you fire off the punches. Then switch over to kicking, alternating front kicks with roundhouse kicks. Finally, combine both punches and kicks together and keep going until you build up a fine old sweat.

The effect of this is to increase your heart rate over a period of time and provided that period is long enough, e.g. above 12 minutes, then your heart muscle will begin to adapt. After six weeks or so, your heart will be beating more forcefully and pumping a greater volume of blood through your lungs to the working muscles.

Aerobic fitness can be improved by any activity which can be sustained for between 12–20 minutes, so by all means jog, swim, or cycle if you prefer.

TUESDAY

INTERMEDIATE TECHNIQUES

Hand techniques

Back fist

Back fist is a circular technique that impacts with the top of the index and middle finger knuckles. It can be used in two different ways.

Horizontal back fist can be practised from a back stance (Figure 18). To take up this stance, begin from ready stance and:

- slide forward a pace on your left leg;
- bring your left leg inwards slightly, so there is no sidestep in the stance;
- keep 70 per cent of your bodyweight over the right foot;
- rotate the right foot until it faces 90 degrees from straight ahead;
- bend your right knee so it overlies the toes;
- the left knee bends naturally;
- the hips and shoulders face 90 degrees from forwards-facing.

Figure 18   Move bodyweight back over the rear foot.

TUESDAY

Once you have adopted the correct stance:

- bend your left elbow and bring the fist palm-downwards against your right shoulder;

- extend your right fist forward beneath the left arm, and turn the fist palm-downwards (Figure 19);

- pull back your right fist to the ribs and turn it palm-upwards;

- use this action to help power a left back fist into the side of the opponent's head (Figure 20).

The striking forearm rotates strongly as it extends and the fist spasm-closes on impact. Use natural muscular elasticity to snap the spent fist back afterwards.

Trouble Shooting

Problems	Resolutions
The striking action is slow and ponderous.	Back fist is a fast, snapping strike. Aim for speed rather than power.
The striking action is unfocused.	Did you rotate your forearm and clench your fist immediately prior to impact?

Figure 19   Take your left fist back over your right shoulder and extend the right forwards.

Figure 20   In one combined action, draw back your left fist and strike with the right.

Figure 21   Lead with the right hand and draw the left to your left ear.

Figure 22   Draw back your right hand and strike forward with back fist.

Vertical back fist is used from close range. Begin from ready stance, then:

- take a half pace forwards with your left foot;
- move all your weight over the left foot;
- bring your right foot forward until the knee presses into the back of the left calf;
- lift your right heel off the floor.

This is known as 'x' stance. Practise moving quickly forward into it and as you do:

- lead with your right hand and turn it palm-downwards;
- bring the left fist to your left ear (Figure 21);
- draw back and rotate your right fist;
- strike forward with your left fist, rotating it just before impact (Figure 22).

Hammer fist

Hammer fist uses the little finger edge of the rolled fist as a club. We have already come across it as part of a lower block, but it can also be used as a strike.

Figure 23   Extend your left hand forward and down, bringing the right fist to your ear.

Begin from left fighting stance, lean forward and:

● extend your left arm and turn the hand palm-forwards;

● bring the right fist back to your ear (Figure 23);

● strongly pull the left arm back to your hip as you strike into the opponent's collar bone (Figure 24).

Trouble Shooting

Problems
The strike is unfocused.

The strike is weak.

Resolutions
Use delayed rotation of the forearm and spasm-closure of the fist to give it definition.

Use strong hip twist and pull back to help develop maximum impact.

Figure 24   Draw back your left hand and strike downwards onto the opponent's collar bone.

TUESDAY

You can also use hammer fist in a reverse striking action to the opponent's head (Figures 25 and 26).

Figure 25   Bring your right fist to your left ear and extend the left arm.

Figure 26   Draw back your left arm, using this action to power a hammer fist to the side of the opponent's head.

Figure 27   Use hip twist to help thrust out your palm heel.

Palm heel

Palm heel applies the base of the palm to the opponent's jaw.

Fold your fingers down to the palm and draw the wrist back.

Press the thumb into the side of the hand. Stand close to the opponent in left walking stance. Then:

- pull your left leading guard back;
- use this action to help power a straight palm heel thrust into the opponent's jaw (Figure 27).

The action is similar to that used for the practical reverse punch. Make the strike more powerful by moving your bodyweight behind it.

TUESDAY

Blocking techniques

Inner forearm block

Inner forearm block uses the little finger side of the forearm to smash an incoming technique to the side. Begin from left forward stance and:

- advance into right forward stance;

- extend your left arm forward, turning the palm-downwards;

- bring the right arm back to your ear, as though saluting (Figure 28);

- pull back your left arm, turning it palm-upwards as it comes to rest on the hip;

- use this action to help power a strong block that sweeps the front of your body (Figure 29).

Bend your elbow 90 degrees, so your fist is at shoulder height. Keep the elbow close to your ribs.

Figure 28   Extend your left arm and bring the right back to your ear.

Figure 29   Pull your left fist back to the hip, using this action to help power the block.

TUESDAY

Trouble Shooting

Problems	Resolutions
The block lacks sharpness.	Rotate your forearm strongly and spasm-close your fist as the block completes.
The opponent's punch is knocked down into your stomach.	You did not keep your blocking forearm in line with your elbow.
The opponent's punch is knocked into your shoulder.	You did not block right across your body.
The opponent's punch is knocked well to the side.	Do not over block – the minimum effective deflection is sufficient.
The opponent's punch catches you under the elbow.	You let your elbow move away from your body and lost the 90 degrees bend in it.

Figure 30   Always aim to block the opponent's punch in such a way that it bars across his own body.

TUESDAY

Practise inner block together with a turn, treating the slide across of the trailing foot as though it was a step forwards.

When you have practised the block for a while, try using it against an opponent in the following way:

- the opponent steps forward into left forward stance and performs lunge punch;

- even as he moves, step back with your left foot into right forward stance;

- block with your right arm, so you knock his punch inwards (Figure 30).

The opponent continues to advance and punch, as you step back and block.

Trouble Shooting

Problems
The opponent steps on your leading foot as he advances.

You can't reach the opponent's arm with your block.

Resolutions
You need to take a longer step back.

Take a shorter step back.

Figure 31   Extend your left fist forwards and bring the right back to your jaw.

Figure 32   Pull your left fist back to the hip and block across with your right.

TUESDAY

Outer block

Outer block uses either the thumb side, or the little finger side, of the forearm to deflect a punch or strike. Begin from left back stance with your left arm leading. Rotate the fist until the palm faces away from you. Draw your right fist palm-downwards on the hip. Then:

- step up with the right foot and bring the left arm across your chest;

- bring your right arm behind the left so the little finger edge of the first touches your left shoulder (Figure 31);

- step on through with your right foot and pull back your left arm, using this action to help you block outwards with your right forearm (Figure 32).

The block is powered by a combination of pull back of the non blocking arm to the hip, and rotation of the right forearm, so the palm turns away from you. The block will lose power if you let the elbow stick out.

Trouble Shooting

Problems
The opponent's punch hits you in the chest.

Resolutions
Begin to move even as the opponent does and rotate your upper body away, and out of harm's way.

Problems
The opponent's punch hits you on the shoulder.

Resolutions
Block right across your body.

Problems
The block isn't sharply defined.

Resolutions
Bring the block to a sharp stop by rotating the blocking forearm and clenching the fist tightly.

You can also use the thumb side of your forearm to block effectively (Figure 33). Do exactly the same as you did previously except that the thumb side of your right arm touches your left shoulder, and not the little finger side.

Practise both versions of outer block in conjunction with a turn, treating the slide across of the rear leg as though it was a step forwards.

Then practise with an advancing opponent, blocking his arm across his body (Figure 34). It is difficult to do more than one or two blocks in succession because the opponent's longer stance will allow him to gain ground.

Figure 33 Perform the same block but this time rotate your forearm until the knuckles point forwards.

Figure 34 Block the opponent's arm across his own body.

TUESDAY

Kicking techniques

Side kick

Side kick thrusts the heel and the little toe edge of the foot into the target. Practise getting the correct foot shape by flexing your ankle, lifting the big toe and turning down the others. When you can do this, take up right walking stance and follow the sequence:

- lift your right foot and bring the knee up and across your body;
- pivot on your supporting foot so your right heel points towards the target (Figure 35);
- lean away and thrust your heel into the target (Figure 36);
- twist your hips back to square-on and bring the kicking knee back to your chest;
- set the foot back down in its original position.

Side kick is quite difficult to perform and early attempts are likely to be both weak and unbalanced. The trick is to smoothe out the various stages so they all run together. The lifting of the knee and the twisting away of the hips must eventually become one movement.

Figure 35   Raise your knee until the heel points at the target.

Figure 36   Thrust your heel out in a straight line.

TUESDAY

Trouble Shooting

Problems	Resolutions
You cannot raise the kicking knee high enough to allow the foot to point at the target.	Kick at a lower target (such as the opponent's knee) until such times as you are flexible enough.
The kick is weak.	Try twisting your hips until your backside is turned towards the target. Then thrust the foot out.
You fall forwards as the kick thrusts out.	Lean back to counterbalance the weight of your extending leg. Keep your supporting leg bent.
You fall forward after the kick is performed.	Turn your hips sharply so they face square-on once more. Then draw the spent foot back.

Also practise side kick from the rear leg. Take up a left fighting stance and follow the sequence:

● change your guard hands and twist your left foot outwards;

● bring your right knee forward and up;

● pivot sharply on your supporting leg so your backside turns towards the target;

● lean back and thrust your right foot into the target;

● twist your hips back and retrieve the spent kick before setting it down.

This is a more powerful kick because the foot can be accelerated over a greater distance. Even so, it is performed in the same way as the first version, with hip twist and the thrusting action combined into one.

When you can perform side kick more or less competently, try standing sideways-on to the target and lifting your leading leg. Side kick slowly to an imaginary opponent's mid-section, retrieve the kick, then kick slowly to the opponent's head.

Don't set your foot down between the two kicks and aim for a smooth but slow action. Hold on to the back of a chair until your balance is good enough to allow you to perform the double kick while free standing.

Back kick

Think of back kick as an extreme form of side kick. It uses the same foot shape and combines hip rotation with a straight thrust of the kicking leg. Begin from left fighting stance and:

- turn your hips strongly to the right;
- allow your left foot to move diagonally back and across;
- transfer weight onto your left foot;
- continue twisting until your back is towards the opponent but turn your head to look over your right shoulder (Figure 37);

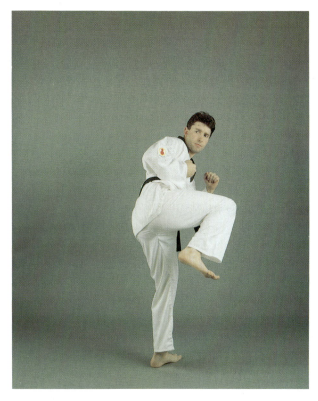

Figure 37   Turn your back on the target but always look over your shoulder.

Figure 38   Thrust your heel directly back and into the target.

● lift up and thrust backwards with your right foot (Figure 38);

● withdraw the right foot and set it down behind you with the heel raised;

● turn your body around and into fighting stance once more.

Energy for the turn comes solely from the hips – not from the shoulders.

Trouble Shooting

Problems   **Resolutions**
The kick goes off to one side or   You turned your hips too far or
the other.   too little.

You missed the target.   Did you turn your head to see
                                      where the target was?

Figure 39   Lift your left knee to kick even as weight begins to settle on the right foot.

Switch kicking

You will seldom kick 'cold' – that is, from a static position. Taekwondo is all fast and fluid action, so any kick you use must be performed on the move. Begin by learning to switch step, and then kick. Take up left fighting stance and:

* jab with your left fist;

* change the positions of your legs, so the right leads and the left now trails;

* then kick!

TUESDAY

All you are doing is suddenly switching from left to right stance but you are not covering ground as you do this. The switch change movement uses a low skimming action – don't jump high into the air. The snap punch helps to disguise your sudden movement, so time it correctly to coincide with the early part of the switch.

Practise switch kicking with both front and roundhouse kicks.

Skip kicking

Skip kicking is a sophisticated way of covering ground quickly and of adding power to a kick. Begin from left fighting stance and:

- jab with your left fist;

- skim forward with your right foot;

- lift the left foot and kick (Figure 39);

- bring the spent kick backwards and down, stepping back with the right foot to reinstate the opening stance once more.

Use only a low skimming step, and don't rise into the air as the right foot moves forward. Time things so that the right foot reaches the spot vacated by the left, just as the kick strikes the target. This makes for a very fast advance and adds a lot of power to the kick.

Strengthening exercises

By now you require a lot of strength in your upper leg and arm muscles to perform techniques powerfully. Train for this with the following programme.

Upper arm exercises

Begin with press-ups and aim to do at least 20 without a break. Rest your weight on the flat of your hands (or fists if you prefer) and keep your back straight as you lower your body so the chest brushes the floor. Then thrust your elbows straight and return to the starting position. Lower yourself slowly, but thrust forcefully back to the start position. This simulates the explosive strength needed to power your punches.

Students with weaker muscles can take up press-up position and then drop their knees to the floor. This reduces the loading and makes it possible to begin muscle development.

Those with good upper body muscles should try explosive press-ups, where force of arm extension is enough to lift the hands clear of the floor. Explosive one arm press-ups are the ultimate target to aim for!

TUESDAY

Upper leg exercises

Put your feet about a shoulder width apart, then close your hands into fists. Bend your knees by no more than 90 degrees, then strongly extend them so you shoot up, and both feet leave the floor. Vary the exercise by kicking on alternate legs as you straighten up.

Avoid exercises such as bunny-hops because they can damage the knee joints. It is not necessary to bend your knees more than 90 degrees to get the required training effect.

Combined exercises

Begin with 20 press-ups, then go on to perform 20 squats. Then aim at 15 more press-ups followed by 15 squats, and so on until you finish the session with five of each. You may not be able to manage this, so cut down the number of intermediate steps.

This programme not only builds strength, it also helps with local muscle endurance. This is the ability of the most used muscles to keep working efficiently in the presence of high levels of fatigue producing by-products.

ADVANCED TECHNIQUES

Hand techniques

Knife strike

Knife strike uses the little finger edge of the hand in a chopping action against the opponent's neck or throat. To form the correct weapon shape, extend your fingers and press the ball of your thumb against the side of your hand.

Take up a left fighting stance facing the opponent. Then:

- turn your hips to the left;

- bring your right arm across your chest;

- raise your left hand to the side of your head, as though saluting (Figure 40);

Figure 40   Extend your left hand and bring it back to your ear – as though saluting.

Figure 41   Twist your hips and cup your hand slightly as you strike the side of the opponent's neck.

- pull your right arm back to the hip;

- twist your hips back to the front and swing your left arm around in a horizontal arc;

- twist your hand palm-upwards and curl the fingers slightly as you strike the side of the opponent's neck (Figure 41).

Trouble Shooting

Problems
The strike is unfocused.

Resolutions
Bring it to a sharp stop by rotating your hand and stiffening the fingers.

The strike is weak.

Use pull-back and hip twist to make the strike more powerful.

You can also use knife strike in a reverse chop into the throat of an opponent who is standing behind you. Begin from left fighting stance and:

- look over your shoulder at the opponent;

- extend your right arm across your shoulders so it almost cups your left ear;

- take your left arm across your chest and turn it palm-downwards (Figure 42);

- turn your hips towards the opponent, draw back your left fist and strike out with the right;

- rotate your right hand palm-downwards and close the left into a fist (Figure 43).

Figure 42 Look over your shoulder and cross both arms over your chest.

*Figure 43   Turn strongly into the opponent and strike him across
the throat with the edge of your hand.*

The hips rotate strongly during the strike and finish 90 degrees away
from the opponent. Both knees are well bent, the feet are slightly
splayed and the knees equally bent. This is known as 'straddle stance'.

Trouble Shooting

Problems	Resolutions
The strike is weak.	You have used only the power of your arm. Combine hip twist with pull-back.
The fingers rattle on impact.	Stiffen and rotate your hand on impact with the target.

Figure 44 Turn your hips away from the opponent and partly extend your right hand behind you. The palm faces upward.

Reverse knife hand

Reverse knife hand uses the thumb side edge of the hand in a circular strike to the target. The hand shape is the same as for orthodox knife hand, except that the thumb is pushed further across the palm. Take up left fighting stance and:

- fold your left arm across your chest;
- turn your hips away from the opponent and extend your right arm part way behind you (Figure 44);
- the left hand is turned palm-downwards facing;
- pull back your left fist, turning it palm-upwards on the hip;

Figure 45   Turn your hips into the opponent and rotate your hand palm-downwards as you strike.

- twist your hips strongly around until they face square-on;
- swing your right arm around and strike the side of the opponent's jaw (Figure 45).

Make the strike more powerful by leaning forward on your front leg as it is delivered.

Spear hand

Spear hand uses the same hand shape as knife strike except that impact is made with the tips of the fingers. Help spread the impact area by withdrawing your middle finger.

Perform spear hand to the opponent's throat, using a thrusting action identical to that used for reverse punch. Simply turn your hips forward and thrust the hand out, rotating it palm-downwards on impact.

Power comes from a combination of hip twist, pull-back of the leading guard hand and a strong rotation of the striking forearm.

Elbow

Elbow is a short range weapon that can be used in a number of different ways. Perhaps the most common is a horizontal strike to the side of the opponent's jaw. Begin from left fighting stance by:

- twisting your right hip towards the opponent;
- pulling your left arm back to the hip;
- sweeping your elbow around and across your upper body, so it clips the side of the opponent's jaw (Figure 46).

Strike with the tip of the elbow, rather than with the forearm.

Figure 46   Clip the opponent across the side of his jaw with the point of your elbow.

Figure 47   Cup your right fist with your left palm and drive the elbow into the opponent's ribs.

Elbow strike can also be used from a sideways-on position. Take up ready stance and look to your right. Then:

- slide your right foot a half-pace to the right;

- bring your right arm across your chest and cup your right fist with the left (Figure 47);

- thrust your right elbow into the target, using a short jolting action. Your left hand adds support.

WEDNESDAY

Blocking techniques

Knife block

Knife block uses the edge of the hand to deflect an incoming punch or strike. Begin from left fighting stance and as the opponent steps towards you:

- step back with your left foot into back stance;

- extend your left arm and turn the hand palm-downwards;

- open your right hand and bring it close to your left ear (Figure 48);

- as weight settles onto your rear foot, draw back your left arm to the hip and cut across with the right;

Figure 48   Cup your left ear with your right palm and extend the left forward in a guarding position.

*Figure 49   Draw back your left and block with the right, so the
opponent's punch is barred across his own body.*

- rotate your palm forwards as the block is about to make contact
  (Figure 49).

Stepping into back stance means that your body turns 45 degrees away
from the attacking punch. This helps the block to unroll.

Trouble Shooting

Problems	Resolutions
The block is weak.	Combine the turning action of the hips with pull-back of the non-blocking arm to make the action more powerful.
The block is unfocused.	Rotate your blocking forearm just before you are about to make contact.
The opponent's punch hits you in the chest.	Step back more quickly and turn your hips away.

WEDNESDAY

Practise knife block in both advancing and retreating modes as your partner supplies lunge punches on alternate sides.

X-block

X-block uses a powerful thrusting action to stop a kick from reaching its target. Both parties take up a left fighting stance. Then the opponent attempts to perform front kick with his right leg. As he does so:

- thrust forward with your right foot and allow your left to skim forward a half-pace;

- draw back both fists to your hips;

- thrust your fists downwards and across, so the forearms cross over each other and trap the opponent's shin between them (Figure 50).

Figure 50   The kick's energy is dissipated by allowing your forearms to slide. Don't lead with your chin!

X-block only works efficiently if you close distance with the opponent – the earlier you intercept his kick, the less power it has. Lean forward and allow your forearms to slide over each other. This soaks up impact more effectively.

Trouble Shooting

Problems	Resolutions
The opponent's foot caught you in the groin.	You didn't close with the opponent, and/or you didn't lean forwards.
The opponent's kick hurt your forearms.	Go to meet the kick and block strongly.

The most efficient x-blocks are applied just below the opponent's knee.

Kicking techniques

Axe kick

Axe kick is an extremely powerful technique which uses both muscular effort and the force of gravity to drop the heel or sole of foot onto the opponent's head or collar-bone. Begin from right fighting stance and:

- swing your left leg forward and up, so the knee bangs against your shoulder (Figure 51);

- arch your back and chop down with the kick.

Figure 51   Swing your leg up until the knee bangs against your shoulder.

WEDNESDAY

Figure 52   The foot is vertical
during crescent kick.

The technique requires good flexibility in the hamstrings. Reach out for the opponent by pushing your hips forward.

Crescent kick

Crescent kick uses the big toe side of your foot in a scooping action. Lift your big toe and turn the others downwards – as you did for side kick. Begin from left fighting stance and:

- turn your leading foot outwards;
- swing your right foot around and up;
- wipe the big toe side of your foot across your body (Figure 52);
- withdraw the foot by flexing your knee.

Crescent kick is performed with almost a straight leg and most of the power is generated from the hips. The shoulders remain forwards-facing.

Retrieve the kick immediately after you strike the target.

Trouble Shooting

Problems
Your foot leans to one side or the other.

Resolutions
Keep your kicking foot vertical.

Your body turns sideways on during the kick.

Keep your upper body facing forward and your defensive screen intact.

You fall forwards during performance of the kick.

Lean back slightly to counter the momentum of the kicking leg.

Figure 53   Little toe edge leads as the foot wipes across your body.

Reverse crescent kick

Reverse crescent kick uses the little toe side of the foot in a wiping action to the side of the opponent's face. Lift your big toe and turn the others down, as before. Take up left fighting stance, then:

- twist outwards on your leading foot;
- bring your right foot diagonally forward and across your own body (Figure 53);
- reverse direction of the foot movement and wipe it back across your body, so the little toe side leads;
- flex your knee and pull the spent kick back before setting it down once more.

Except for the change in direction, the kick is similar to orthodox crescent kick. Keep your kicking foot vertical and your shoulders facing square-on to the front.

Spinning reverse crescent kick

Spinning reverse crescent kick uses a full 180 degrees rotation of the body to wipe the little toe side of your foot across the opponent's face. Begin from left fighting stance and:

- transfer weight onto the leading left leg;
- lift your heel and spin around so your back turns towards the opponent;
- twist your head around sharply to look over your right shoulder (Figure 54);

- draw your right foot in and around;

- continue hip rotation and lift your right foot;

- sweep your right foot around and wipe it across the opponent's face (Figure 55);

- draw the spent foot in to your body before setting it down.

You will notice a similarity with back kick, except that here, hip rotation continues until you are once more facing the opponent.

Figure 54   Twist your head around and look over your right shoulder.

Figure 55   Bring your right foot up and across the opponent's face. The little toe edge leads.

Trouble Shooting

Problems
You lose your direction as you spin around.

You lose balance as you spin around.

The spent kick pulls you off balance.

Resolutions
Turn your head sharply to look at the target.

Put all your bodyweight on the front foot before you rotate your hips.

Flex your knee sharply and draw the spent kick back to your body.

Spinning reverse roundhouse kick

Spinning reverse roundhouse kick is performed in exactly the same way as the above technique. The only way you can tell the two kicks apart is by the position of the foot when it makes contact. Spinning reverse crescent kick holds the foot vertical and strikes with the little toe side. Spinning reverse roundhouse kick impacts with the sole of the foot and the toes pointing (Figure 56) and there is slightly more lean-away of the body. This sometimes gives the kick a slightly longer range.

Figure 56   Reverse roundhouse kick is delivered with the toes pointing.

WEDNESDAY

Skipping side kick

Skipping side kick is performed from a straddle stance.

Look to the right and:

- skip forward with your left foot;
- raise the right foot and form it into the correct shape;
- thrust your right foot out even as the left settles.

Your left foot skims the floor – don't waste time by leaping upwards!
Time the impact of the kick so it coincides with weight descending on
your left foot.

Trouble Shooting

Problems	Resolutions
You land with your left foot, then kick with the right.	Combine landing with thrusting out the foot. Aim at one action, rather than two.
Your body hunches forward as you kick.	Lean back as you kick and maintain an effective guard.

Multiple kicks

Take up a left fighting stance, then slowly front kick with your right leg.
Extend the leg fully, then retrieve it smoothly and, without dropping the
knee, thrust your right foot to the side. Pull the side kick smoothly back,
look over your right shoulder and thrust it smoothly out behind you in a
back kick.

Also try beginning with a roundhouse kick to the opponent's jaw.
Withdraw the kick, bringing the knee across your body. Then thrust your
foot out in a side kick. Drop the foot lightly to the floor and straighten up,
then complete the sequence with a reverse crescent kick.

WEDNESDAY

Stretching techniques

Leg flexibility is an essential part of taekwondo training and it is improved by stretching the muscles. Of particular relevance are the hamstrings and the thigh adductors. The hamstrings run down the backs of the upper legs and the adductors extend down the inside of the thighs. Before stretching either of these, ensure that you are fully warmed up and stop once the exercise begins to feel painful.

Extend your legs out fully in front of you, resting the backs of your knees against the floor. Lean forwards as far as you can, reaching over your toes with your extended fingers. A partner then applies firm pressure to your shoulder-blades, so you are forced further forwards. Try to relax your muscles and hold the point of maximum stretch for at least 12–20 seconds – the longer, the better.

Then thrust back against your partner's hands, tightening the muscles in your backside and legs and really try to force your back upright. Your partner resists you strongly for a further period of 12–20 seconds. Then relax once more and let the stretch resume.

This time, you will find that your fingers reach further over your toes than they did before. This is because muscles tend to stretch more after they have been strongly contracted.

Vary the exercise by opening your legs wide and repeating the relax/ contract/relax cycle once more.

Work on your thigh adductors by lying on your back near a wall. Wriggle your way over until the backs of your legs brush the wall. Extend them upwards and then let them open out under the force of gravity. Try to relax as much as possible and, after a while, you will begin to feel pain as the muscles are stretched. Resist this by lifting your legs against gravity for 12–20 seconds. Then relax once more and your legs will open wider than previously. Repeat the exercise several times, but beware of overdoing it!

Develop dynamic mobility by swinging your legs through the full range of their movement. Hold on to the back of a chair and begin by swinging your leg out to the side, as high as it will go. After 20 swings, work the other leg. Then swing your legs backwards and upwards 20 times but don't bend your knees! Go on to practise axe kicks and complete mobility training by kicking first with crescent kick, then with reverse crescent kick on the same leg.

THURSDAY

JUMPING KICKS AND COMBINATION TECHNIQUES

By now we have completed all the basic techniques of taekwondo, and we can start to do things with them.

Jumping kicks

Jumping kicks are characteristic of modern Korean martial art. They reflect an approach to combat which is radically different from the majority of Chinese, and all Japanese, fighting systems. In a system devoted to the excellence of its kicks, jumping kicks represent the crème de la crème; the ultimate expression of technical skill.

Jumping kicks are defined as those in which the supporting foot is off the ground as the other strikes the target. This means that some of the faster skip-kicks that we have already looked at qualify as jumping kicks. There is one major difference, however, which is that in jumping kicks, the supporting foot clears the ground, rather than just skimming over it.

Timing is important to the success of the jumping kick. The object is to perform the kick as you are rising, and not once you have reached maximum height. All the kicks looked at begin from a standing jump – there is no run-up first.

Jumping front kick

Jumping front kick is the easiest to begin with. Take up right fighting stance and flex your knees. Then:

- straighten your knees explosively and step up with your left foot, as though you were going to put it on an imaginary chair (Figure 57);

- straighten your left knee as though raising yourself;

- front kick with your right foot as you are rising (Figure 58);

- collect the spent kick and land poised in fighting stance.

Aim for the opponent's face or upper chest.

Trouble Shooting

Problems	**Resolutions**
Your kick is low.	Kick as you are rising, not as you reach maximum height.
Your kick strikes home when the supporting foot is still in contact with the ground.	Lift your supporting foot under you.
Your arms move away from your sides.	Keep your elbows against your sides.

Figure 57   Step up with your left foot.

Figure 58   Front kick with your right foot as you are rising.

Jumping roundhouse kick

Jumping roundhouse kick uses a change in rotation to 'cock' the hips. Begin from left fighting stance. Then:

- lift your right foot and swing it up and across as though you were performing crescent kick;

- jump high into the air;

- turn your hips so the left rolls over the right;

- roundhouse kick with the left foot (Figure 59);

- collect the kick and land in fighting stance.

Apart from the added complexity of the change in hip rotation, the kick is basically the same as jumping front kick.

Figure 59   The left hip rolls over the top of the right as you kick.

Jumping side kick

Jumping side kick is a powerful technique that moves both upwards and into the target. Begin from right fighting stance and:

- spring into the air and bring your left foot forward, so your body turns sideways (Figure 60);

- thrust out your left foot (Figure 61);

- retrieve the spent kick and land in fighting stance.

This is a very clean kick to look at, with the supporting leg tucked well up and the hands held close to the body.

Figure 60   Spring up and twist until your left hip leads.

Figure 61   Tuck your right foot up and kick with the left.

Trouble Shooting

Problems	Resolutions
The kick is low.	Get more of a spring and lift your right foot strongly as you swing it forwards.
You land out of guard.	Retrieve the spent kick before you land – not afterwards.

THURSDAY

Jumping/spinning back kick

Begin from a right fighting stance with a strong knee flexion, then:

- spring upwards and rotate your body (Figure 62);
- thrust your left foot out directly behind you (Figure 63);
- continue turning and pull the spent kick back.

This technique uses a combined jumping/spinning movement.

Timing is essential in that the kick must begin slightly before your back turns completely towards the opponent. The extending leg then helps pull you round to forwards-facing again.

Figure 62   Spin around as you jump, so your back turns towards the opponent.

Figure 63   Thrust your left heel out behind you.

Trouble Shooting

Problems	Resolutions
The kick goes off target.	Turn your head quickly to keep the target in sight. Get a good spin-round as you jump.
The supporting foot trails down.	Jump high and pull your foot up after you.

Jumping/spinning reverse crescent kick

This also uses mainly a vertical jump. Begin from left fighting stance and flex both knees, then:

- jump high in the air and spin around so your back turns towards the opponent (Figure 64);
- begin to extend your right foot;
- strike the target with the little toe edge of your vertical foot (Figure 65);
- wind your foot back and twist fully forward;
- land poised and ready to respond.

Begin the kick just before your hips begin to turn towards the opponent and the extending foot will draw them around.

Jumping/spinning reverse roundhouse kick

This technique is performed in exactly the same way as the previous one, except that it strikes home with the sole or the heel of the foot.

Figure 64   Jump into the air and spin round so your back turns towards the opponent.

Figure 65   Strike the target with the little toe edge of your foot.

Combination techniques

Combination techniques are series of basic techniques that are linked together to produce a multiple attack. The reason for doing this is that the skilled opponent can deal well enough with single techniques, but by subjecting him to constant pressure, his defensive shield may break down. Constant pressure means being able to follow one technique quickly with another, so the opponent sees no gap between them.

Effective combinations are those in which one technique sets up the next, so giving it a head start, as it were.

Thrust kick/roundhouse kick

Thrust kick/roundhouse kick is a useful tactical combination in that it pushes the opponent back and into range of a full-powered roundhouse kick. Begin from left fighting stance and:

- bring your right knee forwards and up, so it almost contacts your chest;

- thrust your right foot out and down, striking the opponent on the right side of his chest;

- set the spent kicking foot down quickly and in the appropriate place;

- twist on your right foot and perform roundhouse kick to the head with your left foot.

It may be necessary to skip forward in order to close range for the thrust kick. If you catch the opponent just right, you will turn his body and head into the path of the second kick.

Trouble Shooting

Problems
The thrust kick doesn't check the opponent.

The opponent sees the roundhouse kick and counters it.

Resolutions
Go for maximum impact and try to turn the opponent with it.

Roundhouse kick must quickly follow the thrust kick or the opponent will see them as two individual techniques.

Thrust kick/axe kick

This is similar to previous technique, using a fast skip-thrust kick to literally knock the opponent into range of an axe kick. Beginning from left fighting stance:

- skip forward to close range and raise your left knee to your chest;

- thrust your foot out, striking the opponent on the chest;

- quickly drop the spent foot and axe kick with your right foot.

As with the previous combination, the trick is to run the two techniques together. After the first kick, place your left foot in the right position to set up the correct range for the axe kick.

THURSDAY

Roundhouse kick/reverse roundhouse kick

Roundhouse kick uses a turning motion of the hips, and this is further developed in the reverse roundhouse kick following. Begin from left fighting stance, then:

- twist your hips and perform roundhouse kick with your right leg;

- drop the spent kick forward, leaving your hips half turned (Figure 66);

- transfer your weight onto the right foot;

- continue body rotation, picking your left foot up and curving it around and into the back of the opponent's head (Figure 67).

The point at which you drop the spent roundhouse kick is critical. Drop it well forward and you will close distance with the opponent. Drop it next to your right foot and you will perform reverse roundhouse kick literally on the spot.

Figure 66   Drop the spent roundhouse kick so your hips are already half-turned.

*Figure 67   Transfer weight onto your right foot, lift the left and curl
it around in a reverse roundhouse kick.*

Trouble Shooting

Problems

There is a slow transition from
the first kick to the second.

You lose balance on the second
kick.

Resolutions

Use full hip twist on the
roundhouse kick and land with
your hips already half turned.

Transfer your weight onto the
right foot before you begin the
second kick.

THURSDAY

Side kick/back kick

This is a powerful combination that can drive the opponent clear out of the area. Start from a right facing high straddle stance, then:

- skip forwards with your left foot;

- thrust out the right heel in a powerful side kick;

- only partly retrieve the spent kick, landing with your hips already half-turned;

- spin around and back kick with your left foot into the opponent's mid section.

Building elastic strength

During the course of an evening's training, you may be asked to execute each jumping kick as many as 20 or 30 times. This will make great demands on your physical fitness.

Think of your muscles as elastic bands. Stretch them and they gain in potential power, snapping back when released to give the explosive strength needed for a good jump.

Ask someone to jump into the air and they will bob down first because this flexes the knee joint and elastically stretches the quadriceps muscles on the front of your thighs. When these explosively contract, your knee joints are extended and you leap into the air.

In general terms, the deeper your squat, the higher you will leap – though this relationship fizzles out when you pass 90 degrees of knee flexion. So the first restriction on any training programme you adopt must be to limit knee flexion to 90 degrees.

A few more small points before we look at some training drills. The first is that the bob down must be quick or the opponent will see what you are about to do. Disguise it with a feint or other masking body movement. Secondly, train to get the maximum height/distance from the minimum of knee flexion, so the bob down needn't be so exaggerated.

Begin with step-ups onto a low bench. These work the legs in the right way and are useful for building both local and aerobic endurance. Aim to step-up for at least two repetitions of ten minutes without a break, and cool down between repetitions with some leg stretching exercises.

Progressively increasing the height of the bench will produce a structured training overload to which the body will eventually adapt.

When you can manage 20 minutes of step-ups, then return to the kick squats that we practised earlier. This time, however, try to clear the ground each time you kick.

Split squats are also useful. Start with one leg in front of the other and squat until the tips of your fingers brush the ground. Then straighten up and jump clear of the ground, switching your stance in mid air so you land with the opposite leg forwards. Crouch down and repeat the exercise, aiming for at least 20 repetitions.

Also perform standing jumps, where you first crouch down and then leap as high as possible. Add a twisting component to the jumps, so you spin around in the air. Turn in quarter, half and full circles, going first one way, then the other. The object is to be able to accurately locate yourself in the air as you spin. This is useful because, as we have seen, some of the more advanced jumping kicks involve turning movements whilst in the air.

Then make a series of one legged bounds that take you in a zig-zag pattern across the floor. Leap on alternate legs along a more or less straight line, then walk back to your starting point and repeat the exercise. Walking back serves as a short rest period between successive repetitions.

Start these next exercise drills only once you can handle a selection of those already described. You will need a series of strongly supported platforms of the type you can put together in a gymnasium. Ideally, you will need about three or four of these arranged in a line.

Begin with a standing jump to the top of the first platform. Then jump down, landing on the balls of your feet. Let your knees give under your descending weight, then immediately spring back up to land on top of the next platform. And so on. Walk back to the beginning of the exercise and repeat it. Enthusiasts can repeat the same exercise but this time using alternate one legged jumps to reach lower platforms.

FRIDAY

ADVANCED COMBINATION TECHNIQUES AND PRE-ARRANGED SPARRING

Combination techniques

By now it should be possible for you to perform any suitable combination of techniques and the grading examiner may well make up a series for you to do. In the interim, the following are the sort of combinations you may now be asked for.

Snap punch/reverse punch/roundhouse kick

This is a mixed combination, using linear punches combined with a circular kick. Take up left fighting stance and:

- lean in with your left shoulder as you perform snap punch to the opponent's upper chest;
- pull back the snap punch, using this action to help power a strong reverse punch into the opponent's stomach area;
- reverse punch turns your hips into the opponent, making it easy for you to lift your right foot into a roundhouse kick to the opponent's head.

There is a tendency to throw a light snap punch. This is a mistake because the opponent will ignore it, so aim to drive him back with the force of it.

Your reverse punch travels down from your chin and digs into the imaginary opponent's stomach at just above his belt line. This drives the opponent back against the prop of his own rear leg.

Powerful punches will drive the opponent backwards, but if this hasn't happened, quickly draw back your front foot before you perform roundhouse kick with the right. Loft the kick over the opponent's shoulder and directly into the side of his head.

The examiner may ask you to add a reverse roundhouse kick to the end of this combination. You could only use this in actual sparring if the opponent stepped back from your first kick, otherwise a second reverse punch would be more appropriate.

FRIDAY

Front kick/axe kick/snap punch/reverse punch

We practised the first half of this combination yesterday. Begin from left fighting stance by:

- front kicking with the right leg and striking the imaginary opponent high on the side of his chest;

- dropping the spent foot in the correct position to set the range;

- lifting your left foot high and dropping an axe kick onto the opponent's collar bones;

- leaning forward as you land and driving in a hard snap punch with your left fist;

- pulling back the snap punch and using this action to help power a strong reverse punch.

The opening front kick drives the imaginary opponent back and into range of the axe kick. If you are standing quite a way from the opponent, then it may be necessary to skipkick into him. Though this telegraphs your intention somewhat, the fast advance does add body momentum to the kick. If you begin from the correct range, then you might consider switch-changing your stance first.

If the opponent were to pull back from the punches, then the logical follow-up is a roundhouse kick.

Front kick/jumping side kick

This sequence shows how to fit a jumping kick into an orthodox combination. Begin from right fighting stance and:

- throw a powerful front kick that takes your weight forwards;

- drop your foot in the appropriate position to set the range;

- bring your right foot forward and up, so you launch into the air;

- strike the opponent with jumping side kick delivered with the right foot.

This technique works best with an opponent who back pedals from your attack. The combination of two linear kicks means that you can cover a great distance.

Your front kick reaches well out for the opponent and sets down in a forward position. This, in turn, means that your right leg is trailing well back, from which position it has plenty of distance to accelerate.

The jumping side kick takes a fairly flat path into the opponent's upper chest area.

FRIDAY

Roundhouse kick/jumping spinning reverse roundhouse kick

This is a technically difficult combination that relies for its effectiveness on a smooth and continuous rotation of the body. Begin from right fighting stance and:

- lean back, twist your hips and perform roundhouse kick to the head with your left foot;

- drop the left foot to the floor and transfer your weight over it;

- jump into the air off your left foot, continuing the rotation with your extending right foot;

- strike the opponent in the head with reverse roundhouse kick.

As in the previous example, the important factor is where you drop your spent left foot. Dropping it close to the right foot means that you hardly move forwards at all, whereas dropping it well out in front means a definite advance. If the opponent stepped back from your first kick, then stepping forward is indicated. But if he simply leaned back, then land with feet close together.

Height is important to the success of the second kick. Lift your head clear of any incoming techniques with a powerful leap up. Spin your hips around and extend your kicking knee as far as is necessary. If the imaginary opponent is very close, then it might be appropriate to change to a spinning reverse crescent kick.

Side kick/jumping back kick

This is a very fast combination that works best when the opponent back pedals furiously from you. Begin from a high straddle stance with your left side facing the imaginary opponent (Figure 68). Then:

- skip forward with your right foot in a flat arc and side kick strongly with the left;

- partly withdraw your spent left foot, setting it down with the hips partly turned away;

- quickly move your weight back over the left foot and launch yourself into the air;

- lift your right foot and perform back kick even as you straighten your left supporting leg;

- strike the opponent in the upper part of his chest.

Figure 68   Begin from a high straddle stance.

The key to a successful combination is where you drop the spent opening kick. Land with your hips well turned and you are already half way towards performing a fast back kick.

Remember to quickly turn your head around, so you keep the target in sight.

Pre-arranged sparring

You will already be used to the idea of pre-arranged sparring insofar as you practised a simple form of it during your earlier blocking practice (see page 17). To recap: the opponent performs an agreed technique such as a lunge punch or front kick and you step back whilst performing a block. This taught you how to develop an effective block. Now that block is combined with a counter-attack, to show you how to apply some of the basic techniques which you have learned.

FRIDAY

Typically, the opponent makes three advances, all of which you block in the agreed way. Then following the third block, you perform a set counter-attack. But, assuming you have had enough blocking practice, we can go directly to one-step pre-arranged sparring in which the opponent only makes one advance. You block this and then immediately counter-attack.

Head block/reverse punch

This is the simplest of the pre-arranged sparring routines. The opponent begins from left forward stance/low block position whilst you step back into a left forward stance. As the opponent steps forward to lunge punch with his right fist:

- step back with your left foot whilst maintaining your guard;
- pull your left leading arm back and bring the right forearm up behind it;
- settle into right forward stance and block the opponent's punch with your right forearm;
- pull your blocking arm back and reverse punch the opponent's ribs.

Trouble Shooting

Problems	Resolutions
The opponent steps on your toes.	Take a longer step back.
The opponent overtakes you.	Step back as soon as the opponent begins to move.
The opponent is out of range of your reverse punch.	You stepped back too far from the opponent.

Though a simple technique, this nevertheless teaches core principles of pre-arranged sparring such as:

- moving as the opponent does (timing);
- moving by the correct amount (distance);
- counter-attacking strongly and effectively (focus).

Practise the sequence from both left and right stances.

FRIDAY

Elbow block/spinning knife hand

This simple sequence uses an interesting block and a spinning movement that is so characteristic of taekwondo counter-attacks. Begin from right fighting stance, facing an opponent in left forward stance. He steps forward, performs lunge punch and you:

- step back with your right foot into a high straddle stance;
- knock the punch to one side with your left elbow (Figure 69);
- step around with your right foot and protect your face (Figure 70);
- strike back with right knife hand into the opponent's neck (Figure 71).

The block is made with your left forearm vertical as you lean away slightly. Your elbow glances along the opponent's wrist and knocks his punch off target. Then you spin around quickly, using rotational energy to increase the power of your strike.

Practise the sequence slowly at first until you can do it without thinking. Then gradually speed things up until the whole response smoothes out into a block/spin/strike.

Figure 69   Turn your hips and deflect the punch to one side.

Figure 70   Continue rotation, bringing your right hand palm-forwards to your face.

Figure 71   Strike back into the side of the opponent's neck, rotating your hand palm-downwards just before impact.

81

Figure 72   Block the opponent's punch across his body.

Mid-section inner block/elbow strike

This is made in response to the opponent's lunge punch attack. The opponent faces you in left forward stance and then advances into right. You step back into right forward stance and as he punches:

- step back smartly into left back stance;
- perform inner block with your left forearm (Figure 72);
- straighten your right leg and slide the left diagonally forwards;
- strike the opponent in his ribs with an elbow strike delivered with your right arm (Figure 73).

This technique requires accurate distancing because the elbow strike is a short range technique, and you must avoid leaning into the opponent.

Figure 73   Twist your right hip forwards, draw back your left fist and use elbow strike against the opponent's ribs.

FRIDAY

Mid-section outer block/reverse roundhouse kick

Begin in exactly the same way as for the previous sequence:

- step back into right back stance;
- perform outer block with your right forearm, taking the opponent's lunge punch across his body (Figure 74);
- slide your left trailing foot a half pace forwards;
- perform a reverse roundhouse kick with your right foot, catching the opponent on his ribs (Figure 75).

The key to this sequence lies in the step forward of the left foot because this sets the range of the following kick.

Figure 74   Block the opponent's punch across his body.

Figure 75   Bring your right foot through and hook it back into the opponent.

Trouble Shooting

Problems

Your kick strikes the opponent with your calf.

Your kick strikes the opponent's shoulder.

Resolutions

You have stepped too far forward with your trailing foot.

You have not deflected his right arm far enough across.

FRIDAY

Mid-section knife block/front foot side kick

This is a test of distance, co-ordination, flexibility and balance.

The opponent faces you in left forward stance. Then he slides forward and attempts reverse punch with his right fist. As he punches:

- step sharply into right back stance;
- perform knife block with your right forearm, deflecting the opponent's punch across his body (Figure 76);
- shift your bodyweight back over your left foot;
- lift your right knee, twist your hips and side kick the opponent with your right leading foot (Figure 77).

Range your kick accurately by sliding the left foot into the correct position. Slide it forward if you need to close range, and back if you need to open range.

Figure 76   Step back sharply into right back stance and knife block the opponent's reverse punch.

FRIDAY

Figure 77 *Lean back and thrust your right heel into the target.*

Low block/crescent kick

The opponent faces you in left forward stance. Remain in ready stance until he begins a front kick to your mid-section. Then:

- step diagonally back with your left foot;
- block the opponent's front kick with your right forearm (Figure 78);
- slide your right foot back and transfer your weight over it;
- perform a high left crescent kick into the side of the opponent's head (Figure 79).

Step back on a pronounced diagonal and take up a high forward stance, where most weight is concentrated over the front foot. This allows you to block strongly into the side of the opponent's knee.

Trouble Shooting

Problems	Resolutions
The opponent's shin smashed into your forearm.	Step on the diagonal and block the side of his leg.
Your crescent kick is too close/far away.	Adjust range by moving the supporting foot.

Figure 78 Knock the opponent's foot across his own body with lower parry.

Figure 79 Swing your right foot up and into the side of the opponent's head.

FRIDAY

Low block/step up reverse roundhouse kick

This is similar to the previous technique except that you use your front foot to deliver the kick.

Begin as for the previous sequence and as soon as the opponent performs a front kick:

- step diagonally back with your left foot;
- low block the opponent's front kick with your right forearm;
- slide your left foot directly forwards and transfer your weight over it (Figure 80);

Figure 80   Slide your left foot forwards until the heels touch.

Figure 81   Hook your right foot into the back of the opponent's head.

- lift your right foot and hook it into the back of the opponent's head (Figure 81).

This version of reverse roundhouse is rather different from the 180 degree version which you practised earlier. It is powered by rolling the hips against the movement of the foot, so they open out as the heel or sole of the foot slams into the back of the opponent's head.

Adjust range both by positioning your left foot, and by flexing/ straightening your kicking knee.

Trouble Shooting

Problems
The kick connects with the Achilles tendon or lower calf.

Resolutions
Flex your knee to curl the heel around and into the back of the opponent's head.

The kick is weak.

Lean back and rotate your hips in the opposite direction to the kick.

FRIDAY

Preparing for destruction testing

Taekwondo is interesting in that it requires you to be able to demonstrate the power of your punches, strikes and kicks by breaking wooden boards. To acquire this skill will take longer than a week but, even so, there is no reason why you cannot begin training to succeed at it.

Do not attempt any form of hand conditioning if you are under 18 years of age. This is because people below that age do not have fully formed bones; there are still bits and pieces of cartilage which are all too easily damaged and deformed by repeated impacts. The bone that subsequently grows into the damaged cartilage takes up the deformed shape and permanent disfigurement results.

Assuming then that you are eligible, begin by working out on a punching post – preferably one that is sunk into the floor. The punching post must bend on impact. It needs to be wide enough to comfortably span your fist, and half as wide again, so the need for accuracy isn't critical. Pad the top six inches or so with 25 millimetres thickness of closed cell plastazote foam, and cover this with a tough plastic sheath that you can keep clean.

Face the post and stand with your left leg forward. Take up a normal guard, then turn your hips fully square-on to the post, pull back your left fist and strike the pad with your right. Don't twist your fist on impact – keep it palm-downwards throughout. Don't punch hard at first, rather aim to sink your fist deep into the pad, causing the punching post to 'give'. Try and do about 20 good punches, then switch stances/fists and begin again.

You can also use the punching post for knife hand, etc, but don't use it for kicks because it is all too easy to miss the small target pad and injure your toes or shin.

Massage your knuckles after each session with a proprietary cold cream that vanishes into the skin and soothes it. Use an embrocation if your knuckles become bruised or achy and rub this well in. Then wash your hands thoroughly to avoid transferring remnants of the rub to the eyes, etc.

The object in punching post training is not so much to harden your hand as to get you to form a correct fist with a properly aligned wrist joint.

Toughen your knuckles with a small canvas bag that you fill with flour and hang on the wall. You can use small polystyrene granules as filler if you prefer, though these tend to compress after a time, leaving the bag half empty.

Face the pad in the appropriate stance and begin punching it with gradually increasing force. Your knuckles will become red and sore all over again as they encounter the new covering material and the different target density. Ease this with a good massage after each training session.

After a couple of weeks of hard training, you will find that your knuckles no longer become sore. When this happens, change the bag filling to a mixture of sand and flour and begin again.

Adding larger quantities of sand to the bag with each filling gives a graduated progression towards ultimate hardness. A sand filling will produce virtually all the toughening necessary for the majority of breaking tests.

A gradual programme will produce tougher knuckles in a shorter time than pitching straight into a sand filled bag at the outset. This is because injuries take months to heal, during which time your conditioning programme is halted.

Be especially careful when you have attained this stage of training and don't overdo it. Continuous aches in the knuckles may indicate the presence of tiny hairline fractures in the bones, some of which cannot be seen even on an x-ray. Training through such injury then causes a sudden and serious fracture that puts you out of training for two or three months.

High intensity endurance training

High intensity endurance training means training so you can work at near flat-out performance for a short interval of time. Taekwondo competition bouts last for three minutes, so this is the period that you should aim to work within. There is also a one minute rest between successive bouts, so this indicates the type of recovery period that you must aim for.

The first type of endurance work we did helped us to train at a relatively low intensity over many repetitions. Now we need to work as hard as we can for three minutes only.

Different energy systems are involved in both these situations, and both require different forms of training.

You can use any exercise or training routine, but whichever you choose, perform it as hard and continuously as you can. For example, you might choose exercises such as squat kicks or explosive press-ups. Or you might work out against a suspended bag or pad, raining hard punches, strikes and kicks into it for the set period (Figure 82).

When that period is up, reduce the power and speed of actions, so you are merely moving gently about. This is an 'active recovery phase', the continuing movements serving to prevent joints and muscles from stiffening up.

FRIDAY

Once the recovery phase is over, switch back to full power delivery once again. Repeat this cycle three or four times, with recovery phases between each.

At first you may only be able to work flat out for 30 seconds or so, and then need two or three minutes to recover. Don't worry about that, because with regular training, the body will quickly adapt until finally you are producing a maximum performance for the full three minutes, and then recovering within the one minute rest period.

Figure 82   Launch a barrage of punches, kicks and strikes into a pad.

SATURDAY

ADVANCED PRE-ARRANGED SPARRING

Advanced pre-arranged sparring

Yesterday's pre-arranged sparring introduced us to the notion of a block followed by counter-attack, but in the reality of the competition area, there is seldom time to block. So today we are going to take the concepts of timing and distance a step further – evading and countering the opponent's attack in almost a single movement.

Stop punching the opponent's attack

This training routine will suit the attacking fighter who likes to move into the opponent. It works whenever the opponent is going to throw a kick but fails either to switch stance first, or to pull the leading foot back. Without either of these two moves, the opponent's body moves forward over his leading leg.

You will need to take quite a high stance from which you can explode forward. Bend your knees slightly and balance your weight on the balls of your feet. The opponent takes up a left fighting stance and performs a front kick with his right foot. Watch the imaginary apex formed by his head and shoulders and when you see this moving towards you:

- lunge forward with your back foot and slide the leading foot forwards;
- bar down on the opponent's right shin with your left forearm;
- perform a powerful reverse punch with your right fist into the opponent's upper body (Figure 83).

Co-ordinate your response so the barring block and punch land almost simultaneously. Make sure you are moving forward as you check the opponent, so bodyweight is added to your arm techniques. The opponent is standing on one leg when your punch hits him high in the chest and preferably into a shoulder, where it tumbles him over his single supporting leg.

Performed properly, this technique will knock the opponent to the floor. Even as he is falling, you can skip forward with your right foot and axe kick him.

Figure 83 Bar down on the opponent's shin and simultaneously counter-punch him.

Trouble Shooting

Problems

His shin hits you painfully on your forearm.

His instep catches you in the groin.

Resolutions

You moved forward too late. Move as he moves!

You didn't close distance.

Stop kicking the opponent's attack

This is slightly more difficult than the previous routine, though it works better when the opponent is further away. Begin from a high left stance. The opponent faces you in a longer and lower left stance, and attacks with a roundhouse kick to the head. Even as he moves:

- adjust range with your front foot;
- attack the opponent's ribs with a powerful 45 degree kick delivered with your right foot (Figure 84).

This counter has a devastating effect on the attacker, spinning him and knocking him backwards to the mat. The opponent's roundhouse kick means that his chest turns right across your line of fire and presents a broad target. Adjust both your line and distance by moving the front foot.

Figure 84   Simultaneously attack the opponent's ribs with a 45 degree kick.

SATURDAY

Reverse lower block/reverse roundhouse kick

The first two techniques stopped the opponent's attack before it could fully develop. This technique counters the opponent as his technique is developing maximum power.

Take up a high, mobile stance whilst the opponent is in a longer and lower left stance. Look for the opponent's forward movement as he front kicks, then:

- slide diagonally back and to the left, so the kick goes past your ribs;
- thrust your right guarding hand downwards and lean away from the opponent's kick (Figure 85);

Figure 85   Slide diagonally back from the kick and deflect it with lower parry.

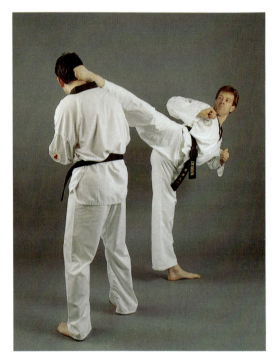

Figure 86   Step up and perform a reverse roundhouse kick, hooking your foot into the back of the opponent's head.

- step up with your left leg and perform reverse roundhouse kick into the back of the opponent's head (Figure 86).

This sequence only works if you move early enough because once the opponent is committed to the front kick, he is not able to do anything else until that technique has been retrieved.

Trouble Shooting

Problems	**Resolutions**
You are too close to the opponent to kick.	You didn't step back far enough.
The kick is too slow.	Lift your kicking foot even as you step forward.

Forearm deflection/reverse roundhouse kick

This technique is also applied as the opponent attacks. In this case, he faces you in a high left straddle stance. Take up a left walking stance. The opponent skips forward and attempts to perform a side kick with his left foot. You respond by:

- stepping back and around with your left foot;
- turning your hips to the left and brushing the kick away with your right forearm (Figure 87).
- sliding forward with your left leg;
- kicking into the side of the opponent's face with right reverse roundhouse kick (Figure 88).

Figure 87   Step back and around with your left foot, turning your hips and brushing the opponent's kick to one side.

Figure 88   Step up with your left and hook your right foot up and back, into the opponent's face.

Trouble Shooting

Problems

The side kick catches you in the ribs.

The second kick is difficult to perform.

Resolutions

Step back **and around** with your left foot, so as to take your body out of the line of the kick.

Slide your left foot forward and transfer more weight on to it.

Spinning reverse roundhouse kick

This counter can be applied with spectacular results as the opponent is in the middle of performing a roundhouse kick to your head. It can also be used by the defensive fighter to attack the opponent as he is retrieving a spent technique.

The opponent faces you in right fighting stance. Take up right fighting stance and watch his apex for signs of committed movement. He performs a roundhouse kick with his left foot and you:

- lean back, so the foot passes over your head (Figure 89);

- then perform a spinning reverse roundhouse kick with your left foot, striking the opponent on the back of his head (Figure 90).

Timing is essential in that your latest attack is made while the opponent is retrieving his. Don't wait until his defensive screen is operating once more!

Figure 89   Dodge the opponent's roundhouse kick.

Figure 90   Spin right around and perform reverse roundhouse kick to the opponent's head.

Trouble Shooting

Problems

The roundhouse kick connects with your jaw.

The opponent blocks your kick.

Resolutions

Lean right back, away from the opponent's foot.

Launch your counter whilst the opponent's kick is still in flight.

SATURDAY

Destruction testing

Twelve inch shelving is the best wood to begin destruction testing with, though you can make do with eleven or ten inch shelving. Saw the shelving into oblongs; if it's 12 inches wide, then cut 10 inch oblongs. Never cut the pieces square or you may fail to line up the grain when breaking two or more boards.

The wood must be dry. That which has stood in the rain for a couple of months loses its brittleness and even wood that you could normally break without so much as a second thought becomes almost impossible. Reduce the amount of pieces to be broken by half if the wood is wet.

Normally wooden boards are held by a number of helpers. Get them to hold the boards with a palm heel-type grip, hooking their fingers over the edge of the board only so much as is necessary to locate it. Don't let them extend their fingers into the target area, especially when you are using kicks.

Figure 91   Aim to strike through the board.

SATURDAY

The board must be presented at right angles to the impact. Assuming a straight punch is to be used, have your helpers stand, one in left forward stance, the other in right stance with the leading knees next to each other. Then have them lean forward slightly and fully straighten their arms, locking the elbows straight. Provide for a slight upwards movement on impact by having one or two additional helpers standing to each side and gripping the boardholders' wrists.

Test your helpers by giving the boards a couple of half-hearted thumps. The helpers should tighten up as they see the punch coming, then relax immediately after impact.

Strike the board hard, aiming to punch, kick, or strike clean through it (Figure 91). Try to imagine that the board isn't there and that may help to reduce the instinctive slowing that can sometime spoil a break.

If your first punch fails to break the board, don't be tempted to try a second punch. If the board appears totally undamaged, then put it to one side and select another.

Speed and skill training

Speed training

Speed training means moving the limbs at maximum velocity, so take great care not to damage your joints. Warm-up thoroughly before speed training and don't speed train with tired muscles.

Wrist and ankle weights are very good for speed training because they are quite light and the effects of their negligible momentum does not show itself in obvious and unwelcome technique modifications. Heavy boots are another way of lightly loading the leg muscles during kicks – though these must always be brought to a stop by a suitable kicking bag. Work out on the bag with these weights, aiming to make your techniques as fast as possible.

You can also use normal weights, but always choose a very light loading and exercise at maximum speed. Try light weights in conjunction with the bench press and squat kicking exercises.

Yet another way of increasing limb speed is sparring in water that reaches your waist.

Improve whole body speed by means of harness sprints. Your partner curls a belt around your chest and holds on to both ends. You lunge forwards and drag him along behind you. You can also run through waist deep water, or sprint up sand dunes. But whichever exercises you choose, practise them at full speed.

SATURDAY

Improve your reaction time by having your partner use a target mitt. He holds this face down against his thigh, and then lifts it for you to hit. Either the pad faces you square-on, in which case you punch it, or he turns it sideways-on to you, in which case you attack it with roundhouse, crescent, or reverse crescent kick.

Skill training

Skill training occurs when your body is rested and fit. By training in such a physical condition, your nerves and muscles can strive for and achieve correct co-ordination and form. Practise all your techniques, aiming to get each one exactly right. And always stop when you begin to feel tired. Without the pressure of 'just one more technique', you can concentrate on the fine points of skill.

Novices need a lot of correction from the coach in the way they perform techniques but the skilled exponent needs little such feedback. This is because his muscles have learned the 'feel' of a correct technique and this functions as a sort of internal yardstick by which subsequent performances are measured.

A good coach who can spot faults is worth a great deal to you. He is able to see the root cause of a weak technique and put you into the correct position, so you come to feel it for yourself. In the absence of such a coach, use a full length mirror to provide feedback.

FREE SPARRING

The week's training takes us finally into free sparring or competition. These are strenuous activities in which you will not only be obliged to use all the techniques you have learned, but you will also have to demonstrate the principles of distance and timing in circumstances where the opponent is not co-operating with you!

The rules of competition

You must wear a clean training tunic over which a padded jacket is worn for protection. A padded headguard is essential to reduce risk of injury (Figure 92). Men must wear an approved groin guard, but shin and arm guards are optional. Fitted gumshields are also optional.

You may not wear rings, necklaces, earrings or bracelets. Spectacles are prohibited, though soft contact lenses are allowed on the competitor's own responsibility. Finger and toenails must be both clean and clipped short.

You will be weighed before the competition begins to ensure that you make the weight division for which you have been entered.

You will be competing in a 12 metre square with either a matted floor, or one of sprung wood. Within this overall area, a smaller square with eight metre sides represents the actual area of combat. You will be designated either as a 'red' or a 'blue' competitor and, as such, you will go to one or other of the two standing points.

Figure 92   You must wear a padded headguard and jacket for competition.

SUNDAY

The match is controlled by a referee, with four corner judges to record the scores. The match is overseen by a jury of two senior referees. These have the power to intervene in the operation and outcome of a match.

Each match consists of three rounds, with a break between each. Bout length is three minutes with one minute rest, though this may be amended by the organisers to two minutes/30 seconds. You must retire to your bench during the rest periods.

The referee will call you to your starting points and after an exchange of standing bows, the bout will begin.

There are several ways in which you can win the match, the most obvious being a knockout through a legitimate scoring technique. Otherwise, you can build up a points superiority. The opponent, and you, can lose through a disqualification – where a serious foul is committed – or by collecting a total of three penalty points. Either of you can also lose by withdrawing from the match.

The referee collects score cards at the end of the match and totals them to see whether there is a clear winner.

If there is no points superiority, then the jury can give a decision on the basis of better techniques or fighting spirit. However, the referee can stop the match at any time and make an award whenever a competitor is withdrawn, or commits a serious breach of the rules.

Each time the referee stops the fighting, it restarts from the same position. The exception to this is when a penalty is imposed. Then both competitors return to their starting points.

Scores are given for clean hits on the opponent's scoring areas with skilful techniques. Straight punches and kicks merit one point, though in a tied match, the competitor who scored most points with kicks will be judged the winner.

Points will also be awarded for legitimate techniques which stun or knock the opponent down. A knockdown occurs when any part of the opponent other than his feet touch the floor. A knock out occurs when the competitor is unable to resume the match after a count of ten, but a knock out caused by a foul technique disqualifies the offender.

There is always a count to eight whenever the opponent has been knocked down.

Points are not awarded if you step out of the area whilst executing the scoring technique, though it will score if you merely step on the line. However, if the opponent steps out as your technique scores on him (providing you are inside the area at the time!), then your score will be given. Points are not awarded if your technique landed after the referee called for a stop.

The referee can disqualify any competitor who commits a serious infringement of the rules. For less serious cases, a one point penalty deduction can be imposed. Three such penalties in a match will result in disqualification of the offender.

Half point deductions are imposed for minor infractions but these too add up, and when a total of three points has been deducted from your score, then you will be disqualified!

You are not allowed to punch your opponent in the face and neither may you head butt him. Groin attacks are similarly not allowed. Do not attack him if he falls over.

Make no sound at all as you compete. Don't grab hold of him, turn your back on his attack, or step out of the competition area. Throws are not permitted.

You can be penalised for refusing to engage in meaningful combat, or for feigning an injury.

Winning in competition

Two things are necessary to win a taekwondo competition:

- the will to win;
- physical ability and skill.

Both of these are equally important. If you do not have the heart for competition, then you should not enter for it. On the other hand, a strong determination to succeed can carry you a lot further than your level of skill might otherwise suggest.

Begin your match from a high stance with a 50/50 weight distribution because this will allow you to move quickly in any direction. Bend your knees and lift your heels ever so slightly, so your quadriceps and calf muscles are stretched like elastic bands. Some fighters bounce gently to build elastic stretch – but make sure you don't become too predictable or regular in your habits!

Facing the opponent full-on gives you the widest choice of techniques, though it also means that you are giving him a nice large target to aim at. Standing sideways-on in a high straddle stance reduces your target profile but it also pulls your trailing foot and fist back from where the action is. Compromise by turning your hips 45 degrees away from the opponent.

Keep your guard hands moving about, so no clear target is presented over periods of time. Take your forward guard out and towards the opponent, where it can spoil his attack close to its source. Bring your rear guard hand back to your chin where it can be used to deliver a powerful reverse punch.

Always keep to the outside of the opponent's leading foot, turning your own body so the centre line directly faces him. By doing this, you will be able to use all your body weapons while he must first make a small stance correction.

Is the opponent taller than you? If so, keep close to him, where his longer reach is of no advantage. Is he shorter? Then keep drawing back your front foot to open range. Does the opponent favour one side more than another? If so, change your stance to match him, even if this means fighting from a southpaw position with your right foot and right guard hand both leading. Remember always to move to his closed side, where his trailing hand and foot cannot quickly reach you.

Deliver your kicks with a switch-change action, using the slight knee flexion to give you a useful 'spring'. Close distance quickly with a skipping action. Check the opponent's advance with a front thrusting kick and lean back as you counter with roundhouse kick, so your knee comes across the body and acts as a bar against the opponent's sudden advance.

Open range before you kick by drawing back your front foot a half-pace or so, then kick with the trailing leg.

Try to give as little clue as possible about the technique you intend using. Begin with what looks like a front kick, but suddenly turn your hips and loft the foot into a high roundhouse kick into the side of the opponent's head. Throw a really hard reverse punch into the opponent's mid-section, so your back foot lifts off the floor. Then bring it around in a full power roundhouse kick.

Swamp the opponent's defensive screen with a combination of techniques. Mix linear with circular kicks and go for widely separated targets. Run your techniques close to each other, so the opponent is under constant pressure.

Turn the opposite way to the opponent such that if he is in left stance and performs a roundhouse kick to your head with his right foot, respond with a jumping spinning reverse crescent or roundhouse kick with your left. Switch change your stance if you are wrong-footed to start with.

Future development of your taekwondo practice

Though this book covers a lot of ground, it will never (and is not intended to) replace supervised coaching in a good club. Without proper feedback from a coach, your techniques will never become as good as they would otherwise. So use this book to get a bit of a headstart on your practice.

Safe training!

GLOSSARY

Although the Korean names for the various techniques vary slightly between different taekwondo schools, the following are those which are most commonly encountered. Learn these and you will be able to understand what is being asked of you in any training hall.

An marki   inner block
Annun sogi   straddle stance
An palja sogi   ready stance
Anuro marki   inward travelling block
Apcha busigi   front snap kick
Ap chagi   front kick
Apchook   ball of foot
Ap choomuk   front fist
Ap koobi   lunge punch
Ap sogi   short forward stance
Arae   lower stomach and groin area
Arae marki   lower block

Bakuro marki   outward travelling block
Balbadak   inside edge of foot
Bal deung   instep
Balkal   outside edge of foot
Bal twikumchi   heel
Bam joomeok   one knuckle punch
Bandae chirugi   lunge punch
Bandae dollyo chagi   reverse roundhouse kick
Bandal chagi   crescent kick
Bandal son   reverse knife hand
Ban jayoo daeryon   semi-free sparring
Baro jireugi   reverse punch
Batang son   palm heel

Chagi   kick
Cha jireugi   thrusting kick
Chang kwon   palm heel
Charyot seogi   attention stance
Chigi   striking technique
Chireugi   thrusting technique
Chojum   focus
Chookyo marki   head block
Choongdan   mid-section of body

GLOSSARY

Daebee   position of the guarding hands
Daeryon   sparring
Deemyun chagi   flying kick
Deung joomeuk   back fist
Dobok   training tunic
Dojang   training hall
Dolgi   turning
Dollyo chagi   roundhouse kick
Dora   turn
Dung sonkal   ridge hand
Dwi chagi   back kick
Dwit koobi   back stance

Fugul   back stance

Goman   stop
Gungul seogi   walking stance
Gup   coloured belt grades

Hardan   lower stomach and groin area
Hardan marki   lower block
Hogoo   fighting armour
Hyung   pattern

Ilbo daeryon   one step sparring

Jireugi   striking technique
Jokdo   little finger edge of foot
Joochoom seogi   high straddle stance
Joomuk   fist
Junbi   ready
Junbi seogi   ready stance

Kihap   shout
Kima seogi   straddle stance
Kyokpa   breaking techniques

Marki   block
Mit choomuk   hammer fist
Momdollyo chagi   spinning back kick
Momtong marki   mid-section block
Mooreup   knee

Najunde   lower stomach and groin area
Nopunde   upper body and head
Nopunde marki   high block

GLOSSARY

Olly o-chigi   upwards-travelling elbow strike

Palkoop   elbow
Palkoop chigi   elbow strike
Parro   return to ready stance
Poomse   pattern
Pyonson keut   spear hand

Sabumnim   instructor
Sambo daeryon   three step sparring
Sandan marki   upwards block
Seogi   stance
Shejak   begin
Simsa   grading test
Sonkal   knife hand
Sonnal marki   knife block
Sudo   knife hand strike

Taekwondo   foot/fist art

Yaksok daeryon   pre-arranged sparring
Yeop chagi   side kick
Yeopeuro chigi   horizontal elbow strike
Yonsok   combination